Prayers of the Heart

Contemporary Prayers for
Contemporary People

John Kane Schaal

ISBN 978-1-63630-188-4 (Paperback)
ISBN 978-1-63630-189-1 (Digital)

Covenant Books, Inc.
11661 Hwy 707
Murrells Inlet, SC 29576
www.covenantbooks.com

To my mother, Kate Kane Schaal.
She was the embodiment of faith, altruism, and love.
Her life was one of continuous prayer—
never doubting, always trusting!
May her spirit of generosity, her loving energy,
and her connection to Jesus
unite all of us as we attempt to connect with our God!

Rest in peace, Mom—until I see you again!

Contents

Introduction

Prayer is the ultimate means of connecting with our God. In this book, my hope is you will find a deep and effective way in speaking with your God.

In our contemporary world, there are so many issues, subjects, worries, and fears that we want to pray about, but we cannot find the words. This book will broach some of those subjects and lead the reader to new and innovative ways of thinking, praying, and letting go of that which we cannot control.

Rooted in our Christian tradition, this book unites us with our brothers and sisters who need our prayers and support. The exercise of praying helps bring about a new metanoia and leads us to new ways of praying.

These prayers are an added catalyst to your prayer life, meant to guide you and serve as a connection with God, self, and community.

This ongoing conversion of Spirit is our ultimate call to holiness. Whether the reader is young, a senior, or somewhere in between, God seeks you out. It is in prayer and meditation that we speak and we listen; and in our heart of hearts, we discern.

This book encompasses prayers for anyone desiring a deeper connection to God. The prayers are organic in nature and come from the heart of the author, who, like most people, struggles with the right words.

However, in this writing, I have felt my own resistance to prayer and ongoing conversion taking place. I just kept praying! My life is different! I feel compelled, despite the personal nature of these prayers, to share these prayers. So please be at peace in your prayer and know God seeks each of us out in unique and wonderful ways.

When we put our fists down, our hands can open in prayer, and we can hand everything over trusting in our God, who creates each of us from love!

Prayer in Times of Frustration

Source of all Creation,
of everything that is good and holy,
beautiful and broken,
distant yet close, please hear my prayer!

It comes from fear:
fear of the unknown, fear of the outcome,
and a lack of control.

And in knowing that I have a reasonable perspective, I have hope!
However, I still feel frustrated, alone, scared,
and at times selfish, angry, hateful, and spiteful.

I don't know whether I am coming or going,
and at times, I don't even care.
I believe in the desire to connect with You,
that I am trying to become whole
while a fragment of me is basking in the chaos of uncertainty.

And so I come before You,
I pause, I thank, I interrupt my day with You!
It's so much easier,
but I often forget.

The road of self-destruction,
where in an instant,
in a word, or a gesture I am disconnected from You
—are my longing times.
These are the times where I am disconnected from You!

In my prayer, I ask only to be intimately connected to You.
Even in my frustration, pain, loneliness, and real isolation,

I can come to You.
YOU are always there with consistency, offering unconditional love
and forgiveness.

On this day, smelling of fresh cut grass,
with the obvious signs of spring in the forsythia and blooming
flowers;
and as the brown grass struggles to turn green, I find You.
I find You six feet away at the grocery store,
and six feet away at the pharmacy—
You are there for me!

This is the connection I need these days:
to find You in everything.
This is my prayer; it is the only answer!

Quieting the Mind

I come before You in confusion,
with a mind swirling out of control.
It seems the winds of chaotic discourse lives in my consciousness,
and it is winning!
Your absence is felt deeply, but I know You are there!

Just how do I end up here, God?
What is this futile thinking that leads me on a path of hopelessness?
In my heart, I know You are there all the time.
What precipitates these moments, and how can I remove them?

I'm crawling to You, God, on my knees,
seeking only your love and direction.
Help me up!
Lift me up to see the hope in the power of letting go and trusting
You!

Give me all of your love, as much as I possibly can let in.
Lend me a Spirit to forgive myself,
to love myself,
to accept myself.

Lastly, help me to stop doubting your presence in my life.
The idea that You leave me is my darkness;
it removes the light You continually offer me!
Allow me to do this with a Spirit of Gratitude and Humility.

It's all I ask, God!
Hope, Love, Forgiveness, Gratitude, and Humility.
And You are the author of these attributes and so—
in those I find You!

My Clay Feet

They are in the way again,
my clay feet, the ones that dangle
and lead me into the realm of troubled times.

When I start thinking that I know more than You!
When I start to control everything;
when I start with anger and rage, self-pity, and hopelessness,
it is the clay feet that are in charge,
and I am in trouble, God!

Help me, God,
Remove these feet!
Replace them with ones that follow the path of love and forgiveness.
Make my dependence be on You!
Take my need to be right away
and make the absolute ego disappear,
for it yields self-absorption.

Help me to love my feet that sometimes collapse!
They teach me to trust You.
Help me to embrace my humanness as gift:
it reveals the unseen God in our midst.
Help me to rely on only You
and the promise that it teaches me to be dependent, in its totality,
and in its most beautiful form—
on You and You alone.

On Little Expectations

Lord, how can I thank You?
How can I ever have a heart that focuses on what I have and not what
I need?
Help me see that my wants are many, yet my needs are few.
You fulfill my every need.

Lift my anger that rises when I don't get my way.
Open my heart, learning that the lesson is pure
and teaches me to be like your Son.
The ONE who followed your every wish
and did it with courage and faithfulness—
if I could just have a spark of that!

God, give me a grateful heart!
One that sings that it's okay to be afraid,
one that embraces sad times as hopeful times,
and one that releases control and hands it to the hands of the Father.

Let me learn that gradually it all works out,
not in my time but in YOURS.
I am right where I need to be in this time and space,
and I trust You will be with me
until the day I am received into your arms.
For as You created me out of nothing, You receive me
without any expectation but my LOVE for You!

The Special Life

Why is it that I want to be *special*?
God, I don't think I want to be better than,
but I want to be special,
honored by others, looked up to,
cherished, and loved.

I know I only need to look to You to find the answers.
You created me out of love, out of the elements of the earth, and
You desired my presence in this world to make a difference.
You made me Special, yet I forget that.

Help me focus on the NOW.
Help me focus on what I am doing with what You are giving me at
this moment.
Make my every move and word be a prayer!
Make my every gesture and disappointment be a prayer!
Make my loss, anger, sadness, love, hopelessness, and grief be a prayer!

Help me understand that in creating these great reversals, I find You.
It is in these vulnerable times You show me I am special.
You are the saving action
reaching to me at all times to save me from myself!
Help me see these truths as I already have!

Make it second nature for me to turn to You for my desires.
Being special is the act of my creation,
my formation and incorporation into the Body of Christ.

It is the life-giving force
that comes from the mingling of your ultimate sacrifice
of your Son for me;
that's what makes me special.
Nothing of this human existence can touch that.
Help me to see that, God. I am forever grateful!

Kate's Prayer

It is a simple prayer, just like Kate!
Your will be done, in all that I do.
Make me be the reflection of your SON
On this earth in all that I do.

Pour into me the grace that it may spread to all those I encounter.
Instill in me the wisdom to embrace a silent heart
in accepting Your will
and in those actions, others will find YOU.

Fortify me with the strength of your Spirit,
that I may forgive and forget.
So that my witness to You will be 100 percent pure!
Give me the humility to be like your MOTHER in all that I do!
Give me that Prudence, the Joy of Spirit, the willingness of acceptance
that only come in connecting with YOU and trusting in YOU.

I may not like it, but I will be okay, God!
My prayer is that like a good servant,
I can be molded into the person I am intended to be on this earth.
And hopefully by your miraculous works,
others will find YOU in my simple actions.
I trust You, I rely on You, my God and my All!

Prayer for Resilience

Lord, You are far from me,
yet Your everlasting promise rings in my ears.
It offers me hope, it gives me courage, it lends me confidence
that You are there.

God, help me to stand up again.
Help me to face my desires, my passions, my desires,
and help me to learn that they too can pass!
With faith in your almighty power and desire for good,
I bring them to You!

Give me a Spirit of Resilience and a Strength of Spirit,
allowing me to continue to find hope in your message that
"I will be with you always."
Help me to rely on the reality that I am not alone.

YOU are always with me; I just need to turn to You in these times!
And so with an open heart and a desire for freedom,
and for all that keeps me from being holy in your presence,
I offer myself to You; fearful as I may be, I do trust.

I know You will lead me to answers,
and I stand fortified with your Holy Spirit,
facing those things that keep me
from your unconditional love and mercy.
Release me from the bondage of my selfish needs
to a new mind and renew in me a dedication to You!

Codependence

Oh, God, I am so tired.
I am overwhelmed trying to lead my life!
You are my only help!
You are the author of all Peace and Contentment,
so please remove my need to control everything in my life!

Relieve me from the need to react and control—
whether it's people, events, outcomes, or fears.
You have always saved me,
always harbored me in the safety of your presence.
Why am I doubting You now?

Allow me to turn it ALL over, not just the easy
but the more challenging.
Help me to bring those needs to You
and not hold them tightly to myself.
It is in giving them to You
that I am free!

So, Lord, I turn to You today at this moment,
renewed and refreshed to give You everything
that keeps me from experiencing all the joy You have given me.
I am certain that my faith in You
will carry me; I no longer need to carry myself!
I have You, and I always have!

On Being a Good Leader

Lord of all that is good and holy
in this world.
You are the ultimate peacemaker, leader, and nurturer.
I reach out to You in the sure and certain faith
that You will teach me to lead with love!

Remove in me the need to feed my ego
at the risk of leading others on the right path.
Instill in me a sense of altruism,
focusing on others who lead and guide just by who they are.

Remove in me the need to be right
and restore me to right relationship with those I lead.
Help me to listen before I speak.
Help me to look before I judge.
And when the need arises to speak,
that it be done in a Spirit of kindness,
openness, and humility.
May these qualities guide me in leading others
by instilling trust and hope for their future.

And lastly, Lord, keep me ever mindful
that without You, it is all so meaningless.
You heal us, You make us better, You bring us together as One
in sending us the Greatest Leader of all,
Your Son—let us rely on his example to show
us the way!

Prayer for Releasing Toxic People from Our Lives

God of all Creation,
of all that is good and holy,
help me to release all things toxic from my life,
but especially those persons who keep me from being more like You.

Teach me to let go, detaching with love,
releasing others with permanence and kindness,
with forgiveness and an open heart that is loving.

Give me the strength to see the reality of toxicity
and its power over my dedication to the building of
the kingdom of love and connection
that You desire on this earth.

Help me to be aware that toxic people need prayer.
They are sick, Lord!
They are creatures of habits that bring themselves and others down.
Make me aware of their weakness, not to judge but to support in prayer.

Lastly, God of all love,
teach me that in making good choices with the people in my life,
it ultimately brings me closer to You.

Give me shared values, recognizing that
we are all created in the image and likeness of God;
and as such, all people deserve love and respect.
So, God, teach me to detach now, for my sake, for your purpose,
and for a healthy spiritual life.
I ask this all with a trusting and humble heart!

In Times of Uncertainty

I am afraid.
I am without trust!
I am far from You, or at least it feels that way.
Show me the way!

Lead me down the path the Psalmist speaks of,
where water will refresh me and lift all my fears.
Lead me to the place where I see You clearly,
where I smile, have joy and contentment despite the uncertainty.
I ask this not only for me but for all those suffering with
uncertainty and questioning your presence in their life.

Remind us that we are not forsaken, God, but it feels like we are!
May our lives be an example of your presence in each of us!
Take doubt away; it is rooted in negativity and fear.
Take apathy away and replace it with unconditional love.

For all of our brothers and sisters who are now living in fear,
give all a grateful heart, one that is so aware
of your magnificent creation and sees You in every bird in the sky,
every teardrop that falls from a child's eye,
and every last breath given
to those suffering.

I find You in all these places because You are everything!
And everything You do is good and holy,
and I rely on that for my faith
even when I don't understand.

In Times of Loss

Lord, my heart is heavy.
I am exhausted with loss and grief.
How can this all come tumbling down before me,
and I cannot do a thing?

I trust in your love, guidance, and presence.
I am in awe of your creation, of the white-capped seas,
your ominous mountains, and the simplicity of the flowers in bloom.
Yet I question, where are You in all of this?
Why have You forsaken me?

I cry out to You in the darkness of my soul and beg for comfort!
I cry out to You in my inability to navigate this grief
and ask for You to ease my pain, even if it's just a little.
Give me a glimpse of your grace and a strength that seems so far from
me.

Instill in me a faith that recognizes that even in the valleys of our
stories
lies a God who loves us,
seeks us, is with us, and shares in our pain.
It is not that You have left me, God.
It is that I fear seeing You in this time of loss.

As your Son wept at the grave of Lazarus,
I too am weeping at many graves,
still missing, still hoping they come back.
Why does Your will seem so hard to understand, God?

Perhaps my prayer should be one of gratitude.
I thank You, God, for bringing them into my life in the first place.
I am not the owner of my loved ones.
I have just received them into my life as part of me,
but, You, God, You determine when people return.

And so I turn my heart over,
beaten and bruised as it is.
I trust that as Jesus promised, "I will see you again."
I know I will see all those I have loved again face-to-face!

Prayer of Gratitude

I praise You, O Creator of all that is Good!
I honor your perfection as I look at our beautiful world.
What wonderful gifts You have given us!
I am so grateful for so much, but especially the gift of your presence
in my life!

I come before You with open hands of gratitude for the ominous seas,
the expansive mountaintops, the earth so rich with your vitality,
that when I try to grasp my hands around these, I am brought to my
knees!

Lord, in your wisdom, You create in each of us a spark of your essence.
We are co-creators in this earth so massive and majestic,
and so remind me to respect this beautiful nature that lies before me.
For every raindrop, every leaf that falls, every flower that springs,
every tear shed, every success that comes to fruition is rooted in You.

God, give me the mindful presence to see You
in every person I engage with on any given day.
Instill in me the knowledge that because we are all created in your
image and likeness,
we are all connected.
Allow that gratitude to assimilate in our world!

There is no Jew, Christian, or Muslim;
no Black, Brown, White, or Yellow;
no straight, gay, bisexual, or transgender—
only people created out of your substance.
And because of that, I am grateful.

Prayer During Times of Loneliness

My God and my Salvation,
why am I doubting You today?
Why am I swimming in the river of isolation and disconnection?
I know You are here, and always have been!

My heart aches with abject loneliness,
and I feel like I am separated by islands from You.
Yet on some level, the idea that I am calling out to You
should help me realize You are closer than I think.

As the psalmist reminds us, Eye has not seen,
ear has not heard what God has ready for those who love him.
So, Spirit of Almighty God, change my heart.
Put me in right relationship with You.
Help me recognize that I need to shift both mind and heart.
From the depths of my heart, I cry to You
for peace of heart, mind, body,
that I may be of service to You.
Lead me to the understanding that loneliness may be my choice
And I only need to look at the data proving You have been here every
step of the way!

Why would You lead me here to drop me?
Or to turn your back on me.
You are not that God!
You are the road map to peace and serenity!

You are a God of mercy, presence, faithfulness, fruitfulness,
unconditional love, acceptance, harmony, right relationship—
always seeking me out in love!
I am grateful, and in the sure sign of your love, I will change;
and things will be more clear, more sacred, more connected,
just because I asked!

I Am Worrying
(Aunt Helen's Prayer)

Creator God, Lover of all good things,
You shepherd me through this life.
Even when I don't realize it—
You are here!

Yet I am consumed with worry.
At times it rules my life.
Worry dictates every choice I make,
and it removes any trust I have in You.
It reminds me of what my Aunt Helen used to say:
"Trust, and you don't worry.
Worry, and you don't trust!"
God, this reminder from my childhood burns brightly in my heart,

The truth brings me before You in a humble posture!
God, I forget these truths, despite your acts throughout salvation
history.
I forget, God, that You cannot *not* love me!
How could I forget that You share all of my pain, worry, anxiety, fear?

I don't go through any of this alone.
In this Spirit then, God,
remind my heart of your goodness toward all creation.
And so, Lord, there is no room for worry, only trust.

Like your faithful servant Aunt Helen,
give me the faith-filled words to ask for your help
in times of worry!
I don't ask for hardships to be removed, no,
but I plead for your presence as I walk through these worries!

Give me the grace to realize:
worry is here and can be gone
just by asking for your unconditional love
and trusting that it will be given.
Blessed be God!

I am grateful, Lord,
that You are a God of mercy and compassion,
and when I have times of worry, I turn to You
as an empty vessel longing to be filled with your comfort!

Prayer for Integrity

I come before You, God, in a spirit of holiness,
in a spirit of reconciliation
in a spirit of somber remorse
in a spirit of need.

I am yearning to be more like You!
I pray for a spirit of authenticity in your eyes in this complicated
world.
In these times of confusion, put a guard over my lips,
And open my ears to your will!

Allow me to speak truth in kindness.
Give me insight into the heart of Jesus's
two great commandments of Love of God and Love of neighbor!
Let those edicts direct my every move, word, thought, and prayer,
knowing that is here I meet Jesus in all those I encounter.

Give my heart a renewed sense of holiness abounding around me.
Help me gain an awareness of the goodness of all creation
and, in light of that, a respect for all created
in the image and likeness of God.

Let humility be the hallmark of that I do.
Let gratitude toward others be the core of my message to all people.
Give my voice a sense of authentic integrity,
seeking to meet justice with all of humanity
so that every person knows they are loved by God.

Allow me to lead by example,
by prudent speech and thoughtful words,
by prayerful presence and loving silence.

But ultimately, God, give me your Spirit of forgiveness
and faithfulness to your Word, and have that word etched in my heart
for all the days of my life.
This is my prayer: to be more like You!

Stop Gossiping Prayer

Heavenly God,
I humbly ask You to release me from the bounds of gossip.
Instill in me a heart that loves, not judges,
and a soul that seeks harmony, not division.

Only when I turn to You and find your face
in every face that I encounter on any given day
will I ever be able to manage this habit of gossip
and putting others down.

Give me the grace to confront myself in midsentence
and change the trajectory of the conversation.
I know I can do this,
but not without your help.

Lord, above all, give me a mindful awareness of gossip.
It is here that my mouth can close long before the words are formed.
And as I try to articulate words of kindness about others,
give me a sense of how much better I feel when I live
a life of holiness.

In return, Lord, I hope to be an example of You.
And as I implement new strategies to deal with this
negativity, make me aware that in participating in gossip,
I am moving further from You and your love for me.

Lastly, as I turn from gossip,
teach me to say positive things when others are engaging in negative talk.
In building up other people in this world,
your guidance helps me see clearly the
building up of the Body of Christ!
May Your will be done in all that I do!

Prayer for Division in Our Country

Lord God, Creator of this magnificent world,
I praise You for the many gifts You have given me and all of humanity.
It is in the living of daily life that I become mindful
of your presence in our world!

Dear God, there is so much beauty,
yet so much conflict in our world today.
The magnitude of this divisiveness is palpable
to all of God's people.

Make us a country of gentleness and kindness.
Grace us with the wisdom of your Word in our hearts.
Nourish us as co-creators of a more beautiful earth,
steeped with your love as our banner of hope!

Lord God, let us use the example of your Son,
sent not to be a King but a Servant.
Make Americans servants of one another.
Let us love our neighbor as ourselves and
quell the division that at times pervades our country.

Let us be willing to listen with intentional love,
not righteous judgement and false egos.
Give us the words that unite those who are
on the periphery of society, often with no voice at all,
and make us whole again!

Take our hands and lift us higher.
Be our light to the nation!
Make us have You as our only desire and
instill in us a yearning to please You in all that we do.
Because serving You is serving your people.

Make us aware of the poor, the marginalized, and
those in need of mental health treatment.
Let no one go hungry or alone.
Heal the sad and those who mourn.
Lift up the ridiculed and hopeless
and make us kinder people.

Let no one be forgotten or disposed of like worthless creations.
Instill in us a gratitude for all life and
teach us to give all life value!
And, Lord, join us as one among many
working to bring your kingdom to fruition.
Thy will be done, now and forever!

Prayers During Divorce/Separation

God, I come before You in total desperation!
Please show me the way to You!
In the midst of this trying time of divorce/separation
I seek your wisdom to follow your will in all that I do.

My heart is broken, and I am walking a tightrope.
Relieve me from all animosity, resentment, anger, and fear,
and allow my heart to focus on You
and your will for me and my husband/wife.

During these difficult days, help me to find Jesus in my husband/wife.
Help me to realize that he/she is in pain as well.
Open my heart to do what I can do in making things harmonious
and help me to let go of what is best left to your wisdom.

In the midst of this dark time, help me to concentrate on the reality
that I am not alone.
Give me the mind of Jesus,
that I may be forgiving, gentle, slow to react, and quick to pray.

Give my spouse relief from his/her broken heart.
Instill in them a faith that we will get through the other side
if we seek You as we discern your will for us,
as we make decisions concerning our future.

Finally, Lord, give us the gift of mindfulness,
that our words and our actions matter!
Create in our hearts an oasis to enter into deeper relationship with You.
In the end, may our vows penetrate any selfish need we may have.
I ask You all this, Lord, with faith in your Son,
who is the author of the ultimate sacrifice!

On the Loss of a Child

O dear God, I am inconsolable.
In your kindness, You sent me the perfect child to love,
to teach, to care for, and now he/she is gone.
It feels like my heart has been ripped out of my chest,
like a part of my body is missing.

I thank You for the short time I had him/her.
He/she brought joy and laughter to all he/she encountered.
His/her life had meaning, and their life changed people.
My little boy/girl was a treasure,
and I thank You for that gift!

I want so badly to scream WHY?
Take away from me any anger I have toward You.
Give me faith that your plan is one of love and that my child is rest-
ing peacefully in your arms.

When I want the answers, Lord,
Give me the grace to seek You out in your Word,
Where You promised that You were going before us
to create a space for us.

Instill in me the gratitude that I was the vessel of your wonderful
creation,
(child's name);
and in that vein, remind me of the joy I was given
while You loaned him to our family.

There are days when I think I will not be able to make it!
Gather me into your Spirit and comfort me with
gifts of memories and the reminder
that all life has meaning, and so did (child's name).

Allow me to find the face of your Son in all those who grieve with me.
Help me understand they don't have the words to help—
no one does—only You!
Let me be reminded of Jesus's words:
"Let the children come to me," and find peace in those words.

Lastly, Lord, as these emotions are swirling in my mind,
grant me a sense of calm.
Help me to see that others need me!
Help me to move forward with this broken heart,
knowing that a piece will always be missing.
But I am better because of (child's name).
Thank You for the gift of (child's name).

Prayer for an End to Racism

Creator of all that is good and holy,
Lord God, hear my prayer!
I praise You for forming me with the gift of breath,
giving me responsibility
that comes with being a believer!

Life is precious, Lord!
I am at a loss in understanding the sinfulness of racism.
As all human beings are created in the likeness of You,
all of creation deserves to be respected, honored, and protected.
This is not our reality, Lord,
and the winds of change are much needed!

In the dark night of active racism,
instill in me the heart of empathy and compassion,
knowing that not all people feel worthy or loved,
trusted or honored—all of this based on their skin color.

Relieve the oppressed of fear for their safety,
trusting that as a community, we are changing,
we are accepting, we are loving and inclusive.
Regardless of color, give all of us insight into the hearts
of those who suffer from racism!

Give us the resistance to speak out to these injustices,
and allow each of us to be a harbor of safety for those who suffer.
Give all who are White, Black, Yellow, Brown, or any color,
a sense of belonging and acceptance.

Interrupt our collective consciousness
that we may be aware that we are all
sojourners on the journey toward You!
Instill in us the knowledge that together we can change.

Give us the insight that the dreams of all persons matter,
and may we move forward
with humility and fortitude,
until that day when all people are treated with mutual love and
respect.

Make this earth a place where color is not a limitation
but a gift, and judgement and hatred
and ignorance of any kind
may be washed away with the gift of Your grace.
It is only with the gift of your wisdom that we may all be one!

A Prayer for Women

Lord God, we praise You for the many gifts You give to us,
most especially those women who walk among us,
serving You in many and varied ways!
They are beacons of light in dark times—and often forgotten.

As a forgotten part of our society,
women are dismissed or unheard.
Change our hearts, Lord. Allow the equality of all voices
to permeate our process for living in this century.

Help us to remember it was the women
who arrived at the tomb of Your Son.
These first disciples had much to say about the building of Your
kingdom.
Lord, remind us the power of their witness
and the power of their evangelism!

Dear God, expand our understanding of equality,
that we may revere those women
who selflessly raise families,
deal with abuse, are looked over for promotions in the workplace,
and seen as second to men.

In a Spirit of humility, allow our world to absorb
the gentleness, kindness, and maternal ways
in which women enrich our world
through their selfless serving as mothers,
sisters, friends, aunts, and professional people.
God, continue to empower women with the voice of reason,
giving them prudent judgement to act before they react
to build a stronger, more loving world.
Give them the continued grace to step out of their comfort zone
and confront the injustices spewed upon other women.

And may they act as healers in a world
that desperately needs them for Your love
to be truly witnessed on this earth.
God, we are incomplete without their presence.

I implore You, Lord, that there be a shift of collective understanding,
enabling women to seamlessly serve
politically, socially, independently
and, with a spirit of true courage, guide our world
to the gifts You have in store for us.

May unity be the motto for all women
and Your strength be the catalyst
for this much-needed change of heart and mind!
May God be blessed!

For Those Suffering with Terminal Illness

Lord God, I come before You confused,
concerned about why some people suffer so much in this lifetime.
I harbor a place of love and healing in my heart for them.
It is often unbearable to watch them live with their pain.

But, God, I trust You, even when I don't trust your ways.
There is a plan, and all I need to do is be present to the suffering!
As You once lifted roofs to heal people, I understand the need to do
just that!
I want to take away their pain and make all things the way they were.

Loving God of all creation, help me to just be
in my uncomfortableness,
in my confusion,
in my helplessness so that I may be Jesus for those who are suffering.

May my heart dwell in your words and promises
that life-giving water awaits us,
a fullness of life which we cannot imagine awaits us.
Let this be foremost in my mind
and the hallmark of all that I do as I minister to the suffering!

God, bless all those who suffer when confronted with terminal illness.
Open the minds and hearts of the professionals
who walk with them in their treatment.
Let these doctors, specialists, nurses, aides,
and all other who serve them
remember the radical revelation of your love in their suffering.

As their suffering mounts and family members
find the visible struggle too much to bear,
give them the heart of Jesus,
who patiently was present to every suffering He endured for us.

Make us mindful of the agony in the garden when Jesus
showed us the ultimate sacrifice of giving up his will for the Father's.
The cup he accepted stands as a beacon of light,
that we too shall rise from the ashes of suffering to a new life,
in a place where there is no longer suffering or anguish, only peace
and light!

And when the time comes for us to let them go,
give us the grace to let them return to You,
trusting we will see them again and that this is not the end.
Merciful God, be with us at these times; they are moments of grace.
They are times of unity and forgiveness, love and hope!
We ask all this in Jesus's name!

For the Loss of a Mother

God, I come before You with a humble heart,
a broken heart,
a heart full of memories and wishes,
a heart full of gratitude and pain!
It almost seems like my world is crumbling before my eyes.

The person who ushered me into this life,
the one who created me out of love,
carried me, and nurtured me,
Loving me even in the worst of times has been taken back to You.

And I find it difficult to let go.
Yet I know that as the Author of all creation,
You determine these things, not me.
I pray she knew how much I loved her.
She was the mirror image of your love for us on this earth—
for so many people!

I thank You, God, for the many years I had her.
As the days went by, I was honored to watch her hands of
love bathe small children, cuddle them with love,
selflessly serve the small and needy
until her work was done.
And before I knew it, I was gazing upon weathered hands,
ones that did your work in all she did had reached their potential.

Thank you for the simple and kind soul You gave us,
giving her the grace in accomplishing Your will
with very little effort, as she wore holiness like a loose garment
because of her connection with You
and your Most Holy Mother!

Lastly, God, I praise You because I know
she is in a place now where love is her journey,
and all of her needs are met.
She walks through the valley of greatness and sees You face-to-face.
She reaps her reward as You promised,
and You cuddle her for all eternity as she rests in your arms until we
meet again.

About the Author

John Kane Schaal holds a Master's Degree in Divinity as well as an MS in Clinical Mental Health, and currently is working in a mental health setting. He has worked in hospices, nursing homes, and gives retreats on spirituality and prayer. John is passionate about spirituality and committed to prayer and meditation. John believes these practices motivate, change, and ultimately bring us closer to our own understanding of God and are integral to our human call to wholeness!

CPSIA information can be obtained
at www.ICGtesting.com
Printed in the USA
LVHW091308281220
674968LV00007BA/571